Isabella

Isabella

poems by Isabella Morra

poems and translations
by Caroline Maldonado

Smokestack Books
1 Lake Terrace, Grewelthorpe, Ripon HG4 3BU
e-mail: info@smokestack-books.co.uk
www.smokestack-books.co.uk

ISBN 9781999674274

Smokestack Books
is represented
by Inpress Ltd

I am a woman and I malign all women,
Fortuna, when I say that you, with a name
like ours, are enemy to every noble heart.
Isabella Morra

Contents

Introduction

I first came across Isabella Morra when visiting Basilicata in Southern Italy, in connection with an earlier publication I'd worked on: a co-translation of poems by the poet Rocco Scotellaro, *Your call keeps us awake* (Smokestack 2013). I entered a small bookshop in the city of Matera, and there discovered the *Canzoniere* of this Renaissance poet. She wrote sonnets in the formal Petrarchan style but with expression and content quite unlike other sonnets of that period I'd come across. When I explored her work further I learned of her tragic life.

In around 1520 Isabella Morra was born, one of eight children, in a castle in a small hilltop village, Valsinni (then known as Favale) in Basilicata (known as Lucania). At the age of twenty-six she was murdered by her brothers in an honour killing. She left behind ten sonnets and three *canzoni*.

Italy was in the period known as the High Renaissance when secular humanism had replaced medieval obscurantism and learning and culture were valued. Artists including Leonardo da Vinci, Michelangelo and Raphael flourished in Florence, Ferrara and Urbino, supported by courtly patrons, yet the South was like another country, socially, economically and culturally. During Isabella's life, she witnessed how, from the hills down to the coast, the land and its inhabitants were ravaged by plague and malaria, poverty and war. Throughout its history Italy had suffered invasion by one foreign power after another, by the Arabs, French and Spanish, often invited in by feuding princes. From 1494 the French laid claim to the Kingdom of Naples, then held by the Aragonese, and skirmishes continued between the French, led by King Francis 1, and the Spanish led by Emperor Charles V, both of whom feature in Isabella's work. In 1513 The French were driven out and in the Battle of Pavia (1525) Francis 1 was defeated and taken prisoner and most of the peninsular fell under the Spanish, bringing to an end the rule of the humanist Popes and ultimately leading to the Inquisition.

In 1528 Isabella's father, Giovan Michele, a highly cultured man and a poet who had supported the French, fled into exile to the court of France to join King Francis who was himself a great lover and patron of literature, music and painting. He left Favale when Isabella was seven or eight and his departure affected her profoundly. At that time he placed her brother Scipione in a college in Rome and then brought him to the French court – where many years later he was to become secretary to Caterina de' Medici. Had she not been a woman, it's possible that her father would have taken Isabella. Like many other noble-born women of the time, she will have had access to the sciences, music, literature including the classics, Homer and Virgil, as well as Dante and Petrarch. As it was, she was abandoned in her castle and her privileged education proved to be almost as much a curse as a blessing. Once her father had gone, the family lands were forfeited. For long periods the family – always engaged in disputes with other noblemen over their fiefdoms – lived in poverty, often at subsistence level, and her other brothers, all younger than her and who maybe resented her privileged education, were left to run wild, their mother unable to control them(*Canzone* IX).

In this period Italy was the first Western European country in which women of means were educated and able to break out of the purely domestic sphere and participate in the social, cultural and political life of the country. Printing had been invented, publications were widely available and women were ambitious and aspired to publish. Prominent women poets such as Veronica Gambara, Vittoria Golonna, Gaspara Stampa and Veronica Franco, enabled by their situations as either rich noblewomen or courtesans, flourished in their cultural milieu. However, unlike other women poets living in courts and cities, Isabella was surrounded by misery, poverty and illiteracy.

The court of Naples would, like the other courts, have been a glittering cultural centre but the countryside of Lucania remained outside time, primitive and elemental. Its customs were feudal and patriarchal and when Isabella's father was exiled, her brothers would have taken over his role in relation to the family, the estate, and as guardians of Isabella's honour.

Isabella was aware of what was happening in the rest of the country, politically and culturally. An accomplished musician herself, she exchanged letters with musicians and makers of musical instruments and also had intense correspondence with other poets and was *au fait* with current literary styles. Her intellectual connection with the life she might have had contrasted with her own physical isolation and will have contributed to her anguish. She was caught between possibilities but unable to realise them. Apart from her tutor, who could this lively, intelligent and cultured young woman talk to?

There is some evidence of two female friends, who lived in the region. One, who is unnamed, is referred to with great affection in Sonnet IV – where there is a suggestion she might have helped Isabella secure a marriage, allowing her an escape from her life. Some have suggested she was Giulia Orsini, Princess of Bisgliano, but she had died earlier at the hand of her jealous husband ten years before Isabella's own death. Her other friend, Antonia Caracciolo, was wife of a Spanish count and poet, Don Diego Sandoval de Castro.

When Isabella was still only about twenty-six, three of her brothers, Cesare, Fabio and Decio, intercepted verses carried to her by her tutor from Don Diego in the name of his wife, Antonia. The brothers, suspecting an affair between their sister and the count, first killed her tutor then stabbed Isabella to death and escaped to France to their father's protection. Two years later, the brothers, together with Isabella's uncles, Cornelio and Baldassino, returned to ambush and kill the count before escaping back to France. They were never brought to trial. Various judicial enquiries and hearings were established following the murder of the count – though not after Isabella's death - but they were inconclusive and Isabella's eldest brother, Marcontonio, the one brother who could not have been involved in her murder, was imprisoned for a month and then released.

There's no evidence to show that Isabella had an affair with the count but there were rumours and that was sufficient. It is possible that she was attracted to the nobleman who was a handsome adventurer as well as a poet – although there's no hint of him or any other man, in her poems.

What we know of Isabella's life is mainly based on the account written by her nephew, Marcantonio, in his history of the Morra family. The ten sonnets and three *canzoni* were discovered when the magistrates searched the castle after her death. So far no other poems have been found although new ones may still emerge from the family archives of local nobility with whom she may have shared her work. 1552, 1546 and 1693, some of her verses appeared posthumously in publications.

Obscurity followed until the early years of the twentieth century when the studies of a dentist, Angelo De Gubernatis, brought her to light once more. Three hundred copies of her *Rime* were published in the early twentieth century and re-published in 1922. Most importantly, during that period she was discovered by the famous Italian scholar and philosopher, Senator Benedetto Croce, who in 1929, after years of painstaking work and what he called 'a pilgrimage' to Isabella's birthplace, wrote a long essay about her life: *Isabella di Morra e Don Diego Sandoval de Castro* which was published together with her thirteen surviving poems and poems by Don Diego.

Although she followed the Petrarchan fashion of the day, Isabella describes her style as rough and unpolished for its relative lack of artifice and verbal ornamentation, and the content of her sonnets also departs from convention in several respects. There are no poems of desire for an unattainable lover, only expressions of longing to be re-united with her father. The dominant and unusual protaganist in her sonnets is Favale. Three centuries later the poet Giacomo Leopardi was to write similarly of his own birthplace, Recanati, and is said to have been influenced by his reading of Isabella Morra. The peripheral and abandoned nature of the land mirrored Isabella's own condition and became the main theme and metaphor in her work, giving it a visual and emotional power. Mostly she addressed her environment in a spirit of anger but occasionally as a friend, or at least a kindred spirit. Other characters she addressed in her work included 'Fortune', maybe easier for a contemporary reader to relate to when understood partly as a representation of the oppressive and malevolent social forces that held her back as a woman at that time.

The longer *canzoni* together with the sonnets give a sense of the emotional trajectory of her short life. Isabella's first *Canzone* is a narrative autobiographical poem. The sensual descriptions of Christ in the second, an intense, religious poem, remind us that she was still a sexually unfulfilled young woman. The other mystical *Canzone*, addressed to the Virgin Mary, was possibly her last poem and expresses an intention to withdraw from the world as a hermit dressed in rough clothes, relinquishing her literary ambitions.

From the eighth century, Spain and Sicily were the centres of Muslim civilisation and its culture permeated Southern Italy, with Sufi centres established across the area. Isabella's poems are written within the Neo-Platonist tradition and use classical imagery, but their yearning for spiritual unity and their sensuality of expression also reach back to an oriental cultural inheritance and echo the ghazals of the great Sufi poet Rumi, writing in the same century, full of a spiritual yearning to be united in love with Shams of Kabriz and to return to an ideal home or heaven.

In my translations I wanted to preserve the formality and elegance of these sixteenth century poems and at the same time to make Isabella's work as accessible as possible to a contemporary reader. In that spirit I have used the iambic pentameter metre of the traditional English sonnet but have often departed from the strict Petrarchan rhyme. Isabella's *Canzoni* have a complex pattern of rhyme and varying syllabic lines with eleven-line stanzas and a five-line *commiato* or valediction to close each poem. I have maintained the structure but have not followed the rhyming pattern and syllabics of the originals.

In 2015 I returned to Basilicata to Tricarico, the birthplace of Rocco Scotellaro whose poems had first brought me to the area, and to Valsinni where Isabella was born. I travelled down from the centre of Italy on the 'Freccia Bianca' – the white arrow, a train that runs along the Adriatic from Venice down towards the heel of Italy. From there I travelled by car across the changing landscape from Tricarico to Valsinni. 'South' starts with my journey towards Isabella's birthplace. My poems are made up of different voices and perspectives, including mine and those of Isabella's mother of whom there is little record and of the poet herself. The real Isabella remains as elusive as when I set out to discover her but her few poems and what she represents are very much with us. She was a young woman, in this case a passionate and talented young poet, caught in a predicament common to many women throughout history across the world who, like her, may be educated and have an awareness of the possibilities their education can offer but are denied access to those possibilities and too often suffer a violent death as punishment for rebelling against the conventions of their family or society.

Caroline Maldonado, 2019

Favale

High on Monte Coppolo
  traces of ancient Lucanians
    and an acropolis left by Greeks;

below, the River Sinni where women
  scrub their sheets
    and carry their jugs

through *la valle della donna* to draw
  sweet water from its source.
    In her Norman castle, Isabella.

A *gentildonna*, her aspiration the life
  of the court, her vocation that of a poet,
    she writes what she knows: herself

and the poor, deserted land, coastline
  lethal with swamps and malaria,
    hills made treacherous by landslides,

forests running with hares and foxes:
  places she curses, then withdraws to.
    From the peak of Monte Coppolo

  she turns her back on Favale,
    her eyes searching the far sea.

CM

Ten
Sonnets

I

I fieri assalti di crudel Fortuna
scrivo piangendo, e la mia verde etate;
me che 'n sì vili ed orride contrate
spendo il mio tempo senza loda alcuna.

Degno il sepolcro, se fu vil la cuna,
vo procacciando con le Muse amate,
e spero ritrovar qualche pietate
malgrado de la cieca aspra importuna;

e col favor de le sacrate Dive,
se non col corpo, almen con l'alma sciolta,
essere in pregio a più felice rive.

Questa spoglia, dov'or mi trovo involta,
forse tale alto Re nel mondo vive,
che 'n saldi marmi la terrà sepolta.

I

I write weeping about the fierce assaults
on me by cruel Fortune and the lost days
of my youth, how in this vile, odious hamlet
I spend my life without a word of praise.

My cradle was cursed but I will earn a tomb
for I pursue a dream with my sweet Muses
and despite the interfering, blind goddess
one day I hope to find pity again.

And by the grace of my sacred spirit, at least
my soul, if not my body, will be set free
and valued more highly in some happier place.

As for this mortal frame that now confines me,
perhaps a great king, elsewhere on the globe,
will have it buried in a fine, marble grave.

II

Sacra Giunone, se i volgari amori
son de l'alto tuo cor tanto nemici,
i giorni e gli anni miei chiari felici
fa' con tuoi santi e ben concessi ardori.

A voi consacro i miei verginei fiori
a te, o dea, e ai tuoi pensieri amici,
o de le cose sola alme beatrici,
che colmi il ciel de' tuoi soavi odori.

Cingimi al collo un bello aurato laccio
de' tuo' più cari ed umili soggetti,
che di servir a te sola procaccio.

Guida Imeneo con sì cortesi affetti
e fa' sì caro il nodo ond'io mi allaccio,
ch'una sola alma regga i nostri petti.

II

Sacred Juno, since unsanctified love
so offends your chaste and virtuous heart,
spread blissful joy throughout my days and years
with the holy passion you generously bestow.

To you I consecrate my virginal flowers
and to your kindly thoughts, O Goddess.
Alone among creatures benign and blessed,
you fill heaven with your gentle aromas.

Tie a fine, gold knot around my neck.
You are the only one I wish to serve,
I am your dearest and most humble subject.

Guide me, Hymen, with tenderness so sweet
and make the knot where I will bind myself
so dear that but one soul rules both our hearts.

III

D'un alto monte onde si scorge il mare
miro sovente io, tua figlia Isabella,
s'alcun legno spalmato in quello appare,
che di te, padre, a me doni novella.

Ma la mia adversa e dispietata stella
non vuol ch'alcun conforto possa entrare
nel tristo cor, ma, di pietà rubella,
la calda speme in pianto fa mutare.

Ch'io non veggo nel mar remo nè vela
(così deserto è lo infelice lito)
che l'onda fenda o che la gonfi il vento.

Contra Fortuna alor spargo querela,
ed ho in odio il denigrato sito,
come sola cagion del mio tormento.

III

From this high peak with its view over the sea
I, your daughter Isabella, often look out
hoping for a wooden ship to appear,
Father, that will bring me back news of you.

But my stars, hostile and without mercy,
will not allow the smallest drop of comfort
to enter my sad heart and, despising pity,
they convert my burning hope to tears.

For when I see no oars cut through the waves
nor a single sail billow in the wind
(the shoreline is so abandoned, so alone!),

then must I speak out against my fate
and nurse my hatred for this forsaken place
that is the one and only cause of my torment.

IV

Quanto pregiar ti puoi, Siri mio amato,
de la tua ricca e fortunata riva
e de la terra che da te deriva
il nome, ch'al mio cor oggi è sì grato;

s'ivi alberga colei, che 'l cielo irato
può far tranquillo e la mia speme viva,
malgrado de l'acerba e cruda Diva,
ch'ogni or s'esalta del mio basso stato.

Non men l'odor de la vermiglia Rosa
di dolce aura vital nodrisce l'alma
che soglian farsi i sacri Gigli d'oro.

Sarà per lei la vita mia gioiosa,
de' grievi affanni deporrò la salma,
e queste chiome cingerò d'alloro.

IV

How you must rejoice, my lovely Siri,
in your fertile banks so blessed by Fortune,
and in the land that has taken your name
which fills my heart with gratitude today!

For she lives there, one who is able to quieten
the frenzied sky and spur on my ambition
despite the bitter, cruel Goddess exalting
hourly over my wretched situation.

The perfume of the vermilion rose with its sweet
and vital aura feeds the soul no less
than does the sacred golden lily's scent.

Joy will lighten my days because of her;
she will lift the burden that weighs me down
and bind a garland of laurel around my hair.

V

Non sol il ciel vi fu largo e cortese,
caro Luigi, onor del secol nostro,
del rar stil, del ben purgato inchiostro,
ma del nobil soggetto onde v'accese.

Alto Signor e non umane imprese
ornan d'eterna fronde il capo vostro,
cose più da pregiar che gemme od ostro,
che dai tarli e dal tempo son offese.

Il sacro volto aura soave inspira
al dotto petto, che lo tien fecondo
di gloriosi, anzi divini carmi.

Francesco è l'arco de la vostra lira,
per lui sète oggi a null'aaltro secondo,
e potete col son rompere i marmi.

V

Not only has courteous Heaven rewarded you,
Dear Luigi, most honoured poet of our time,
with an elegance and rarity of style
but also with the noble subject that fires you.

It is not human endeavour but a great king
who adorns your head with eternal laurel leaves,
things of more worth than either purple or gems
for cloth falls prey to worms and gems to time.

His sacred face inspires a gentle aura
in your learned heart, keeping it fertile
with poems which are glorious, even divine.

Francis is the arc of your lyre,
in his eyes you are second to none
and can break open marble with your song.

VI

Fortuna che sollevi in alto stato
ogni depresso ingegno, ogni vil core,
or fai ch 'l mio in lagrime e 'n dolore
viva più che altro afflitto e sconsolato.

Veggio il mio Re da te vinto e prostrato
sotto la rota tua, pieno d'orrore,
lo qual, fra gli altri eroi, era il maggiore
che da Cesare in qua fusse mai stato.

Son donna, e contra de le donne dico:
che tu , Fortuna, avendo il nome nostro,
ogni ben nato cor hai per nemico.

E spesso grido col mio rozo inchiostro,
che chi vuol esser tuo più caro amico
sia degli uomini orrendo e raro mostro.

VI

You have promoted every minor talent,
Fortuna, rewarded every sordid heart,
you now compel my own, long past all tears,
to face still more hardship, feel more desolate.

I see my king fallen, thrown down by you,
lying prostrate under your wheel, insane
with fear, one who – compared to any man
since Caesar lived – has been our greatest hero.

I am a woman and I malign all women,
Fortuna, when I say that you, with a name
like ours, are enemy to every noble heart.

Time and again I cry with my crude pen
that whoever wants to be your best friend
must be a strange monster, repellent to men.

VII

Ecco che'un'altra volta, o valle inferna,
o fiume alpestre, o ruinati sassi,
o ignudi spirti di virtute e cassi,
udrete il pianto e la mia doglia eterna.

Ogni monte udirammi, ogni caverna,
ovunqu'io arresti, ovunqu'io mova i passi;
chè Fortuna, che mai salda non stassi,
cresce ogn'or il mio male, ogn'or l'eterna.

Deh, mentre ch'io mi lagno e giorno e notte,
o fere, o sassi, o orride ruine,
o selve incolte, o solitarie grotte,

ulule, e voi del mal nostro indovine,
piangete meco a voci alte interrotte
il mio più d'altro miserando fine.

VII

Here once again, O hell-like wasted valley,
O Alpine river, shattered heaps of stone,
spirits stripped bare of all goodness or pity,
you will hear the voice of my endless pain.

Every cave will hear me, every hill,
wherever I stay or my footsteps lead me,
for Fortune, who never rests or holds still,
steps up my pain each hour to last eternally.

And as I cry out through the nights and days,
you, wild beasts, rocks, infernal ruins,
untamed forests and solitary caves,

even you, hawk owls who presage ill,
come howl with me in your loud, broken voices
for what is to come, my saddest fate of all.

VIII

Torbido Siri, del mio mal superbo,
or ch'io sento da presso il fine amaro,
fa' tu noto il mio duolo al Padre caro,
se mai qui 'l torna il suo destin acerbo.

Dilli come, morendo, disacerbo
l'aspra Fortuna e lo mio fato avaro,
e, con esempio miserando e raro,
nome infelice e le tue onde servo.

Tosto ch'ei giunga a la sassosa riva
(a che penar m'adduci, o fiera stella,
come d'ogni mio ben son cassa e priva!)

inqueta l'onde con crudel procella,
e di': – Mi accreber sì, mentre fu viva,
con gli occhi no, ma i fiumi d'Isabella.

VIII

Muddy, swollen Siri, scornful of my pain,
now that I sense my wretched end come near,
let my dear father learn of my despair
if his destiny allows him home again.

Tell him how, by my death, I appease
my bitter fortune and the misery of my fate,
and with the lesson of my strange, pitiful tale
bequeath my unlucky name to your waves.

As soon as he arrives at this stony riverside
(O cruel stars, what you lead me to think of
now I am robbed and stripped of everything good!),

whip up your restless waves with violent storms,
say, I swelled so great when Isabella was alive,
not from her eyes alone, but from her streams.

IX

Se a la propinqua speme nuovo impaccio
o Fortuna crudele o l'empia Morte,
com'han soluto, ahi lassa, non m'apporte,
rotta avrò la prigione e sciolto il laccio.

Ma, pensando a quel dì, ardo e agghiaccio,
chè 'l timore e 'l desio son le mi scorte;
a questo or chiudo, or apro a quel le porte
e, in forse, di dolor mi struggo e sfaccio.

con ragione il desio dispiega i vanni
ed al suo porto appressa il bel pensiero
per trar quest'alma da perpetui affanni.

Ma Fortuna al timor mostra il sentiero
erto ed angusto e pien di tanti inganni,
che nel più bel sperar poi mi dispero.

IX

If either unholy Death or cruel Fortune
should yet again obstruct my rising hopes,
worn down as I am it will do me no harm,
I will have smashed my prison, slipped my noose.

Yet, thinking of that day, I freeze and burn
for both fear and longing are my escort;
I shut out the first only to let in the second,
consume myself in doubt and fall apart.

With good reason desire spreads out its wings
and draws my hopes closer into its port,
leading my soul away from constant cares.

But Fate shows fear a steep and dangerous route,
a narrow path strewn with so many snares
that when my hope is highest I most despair.

X

Scrissi con stile amaro, aspro e dolente
un tempo, come sai, contra Fortuna,
sì che null'altra mai sotto la luna
di lei si dolse con voler più ardente.

Or del suo cieco error l'alma si pente,
che in tai doti non scorge gloria alcuna,
e se de' beni suoi vive digiuna,
spera arricchirsi in Dio chiara e lucente.

Nè tempo o morte il bel tesoro eterno,
nè predatrice e violenta mano
ce lo torrà davanti al Re del cielo.

ivi non nuoce già state nè verno,
chè non si sente mai caldo nè gielo.
Dunque, ogni altro sperar, fratello, è vano.

X

You know, in those days, how bitterly I wrote,
with what anger and pain I denounced Fortune.
No woman under the moon ever complained
with greater passion than me about her fate.

Now my soul repents of its blind mistake,
no longer finding glory in gifts such as these
and though starved of all that is good while it lives,
it hopes to grow rich in the light of God's grace.

Neither time nor death, nor some violent,
rapacious hand will snatch away the eternal,
beautiful treasure before the King of Heaven.

Nor will summer or winter ever do harm,
for there, no-one feels heat or icy cold.
You see, brother, all other hope is vain.

Dolore

Here, *grief*'s the word. It's hard to shift
a feeling across countries, with centuries
in between, and still keep the sense of it.

Sorrow or suffering, sadness or regret?
For the loss of her father and her isolation
and the freedom that, as a woman, she'll

never have (though she knows about it
well enough) and that always flees her, like fame.
For her, *grief* must be the most apt.

She trudges her loathed landscape, searches
the Sinni waters, through mountain mists,
in the tangled forests around her castle

which at least offer shade from numbing rays.
And when she retires to a cave dressed
in coarse cloth, after her sonnets and her *canzoni*

to Christ and the Virgin Mary,
when grief has done its worst and still
there's more to come, she doesn't seek to end
her life, only in silence make it her own.

CM

Three
Canzoni

I

Poscia che al bel desir troncate hai l'ale,
che nel mio cor sorgea, crudel Fortuna,
si che d'ogni tuo ben vivo digiuna,
dirò con questo stil rivido e frale
alcuna parte de l'interno male
causato sol da te fra questi dumi,
fra questi aspri costumi,
di gente irrazional, priva d'ingegno,
ove senza sostegno
son costretta a menare il viver mio,
qui posta da ciascuno in cieco oblio.

Tu, crudel, de l'infanzio in quei pochi anni,
dal carcer duro il vel de l'alma stanca,
del caro genitor mi festi priva
che, se non è già pur ne l'altra riva,
per me sente di morte i grevi affanni,
chè 'l mio penar raddoppia gli suoi danni.
Cesar gli vieta il poter darmi aita.
O cosa non più udita,
privar il padre di giovar la figlia!
così, a disciolta briglia
seguitata m'hai sempre, empia Fortuna,
cominciando dal latte e da la cuna.

I

Now, cruel Fortune, when you have clipped the wings
of that beautiful dream taking flight in my heart
leaving me starved of anything good,
I will tell in my rough, unpolished tongue
some of the anguish caused by you alone,
here in bramble and thorn
among people gross in their habits
who lack both reason and wit,
where with no-one to support me I am forced
to spend my life in blind obscurity.

In my early years you cruelly deprived me
of my dear parent, and if he has not already crossed
to the other shore, he will share the grave thoughts
of death that weigh me down,
for his sorrow will be doubled by my pain.
Caesar will not let him help me.
Have you ever heard of such a thing –
to keep a father from comforting his daughter!
This is the way, unholy Fortune,
you have always pursued me with a free rein
ever since my days of milk and the cradle.

Quella ch'è detta la fiorita etade,
secca ed oscura, solitaria ed erma
tutta ho passata qui cieca ed inferma,
senza saper mai pregio di beltade.
È stata per me morta in te pietade,
e spenta l'hai in altrui, che potea sciorre
e in altra parte porre
dal carcer duro il vel de l'alma stanca,
che, come neve bianca,
dal sol, così da te si strugge ogni ora,
e struggerassi infin che qui dimora.

Qui non provo io di donna il proprio stato
per te, che posta m'hai in sì ria sorte
che dolce vita mi saria la morte.
I cari pegni del mio padre amato
piangon d'intorno. Ahi, ahi, miser fato,
mangiar e il frutto, ch'altri colse, amaro
quei che mai non peccaro,
la cui semplicità faria clemente
una tigre, un serpente,
ma non già te, ver noi più fiera e rea
ch'al figlio Progne ed al fratel Medea.

Dei ben, che ingiustamente la tua mano
dispensa, fatta m'hai tanto mendica,
che mostri ben quanto sei nemica,
in questo inferno solitario e strano
ogni disegno mio facendo vano.
S'io mi dogli di te sì giustamente
per isfogar la mente,
da chi non son per ignoranza intesa
i' son, lassa, ripresa:
chè, se nodrita già fossi in cittade,
avresti tu più biasmo, io più pietade.

That stage of life they call a blossoming
has been for me arid, dark, solitary and bleak.
I have spent all of it here, sightless, sick,
never hearing my beauty praised.
Any pity you had for me is dead
and you have killed it in another
who could have set free from its harsh prison
my soul's tired body and taken it elsewhere,
but as white snow by sun
it is consumed by you hour by hour
and will be consumed as long as I stay here.

Nor do I live as any woman should
for you have brought me to such a state
that death would be the sweetest life for me.
The dear sons of my beloved father
cry all around me. What a miserable fate
to eat fruit picked by others! So bitter
for those who have never sinned,
whose innocence would make a tiger
or serpent feel compassion but not you,
prouder and crueller towards us than was Procne
to her son or Medea to her brother.

And as for the riches you hand out
so unfairly, by making such a beggar of me
you prove that you are my enemy
in this lonely, unimaginable hell
where any plan I make is made in vain.
If with good cause I complain of you
to unburden myself, those who in their ignorance
misunderstand me, alas, condemn me:
for had I been raised in the city
you would have received more blame,
I more pity.

Bastone i figli de la fral vecchiezza
esser dovean di mia misera madre;
ma per le tue procelle inique ed adre
sono in estrema ed orrida fiacchezza;
e spenta in lor sarà la gentilezza
dagli antichi lasciata, a questi giorni,
se dagli altri soggironi
pietà non giunge al cor del Re di Francia,
che, con giusta bilancia
pesando il danno, agguaglie la mercede
second il merto di mia pura fede.

Ogni mal ti perdono,
nè l'alma si dorrà di te giammai
se questo sol farai
(ahi, ahi, Fortuna, e perchè far nol dêi? –
che giungan al gran Re gli sospir miei.

My poor mother's sons should be the staff
to support her in her frail old age, but battered
by your dark, destructive storms
they live in a state of extreme indolence.
Gone will be the civility passed down to them
from the ancients to our own times, unless
pity from on high
reaches the French King's heart
and he, with his just scales, measures the hurt
and delivers mercy, according to the worth
of my pure faith.

I forgive all the wrongs you have done me
and never again will my soul complain of you
if you will grant only this
(Oh, oh, Fortune, why would you not do it?) –
let my sighs reach the great King.

II

Signor, che insino a qui, tua gran mercede,
con questa vista mia caduca e frale
spregiar m'hai fatto ogni beltà mortale,
fammi di tanto ben per grazia erede
che sempre ami te sol con pura fede
e spregie per innanzi ogni altro oggetto,
con si verace affetto,
ch'ognun m'additi per tua fida amante
in questo mondo errante,
ch'altro non è, senza il tu'amor celeste,
ch'un procelloso mar pien di tempeste.

Signor, che di tua man fattura sei,
ov'ogni ingengno s'affatica in vano,
ritrarre in versi il tuo bel volto umano,
or sol per disfogare i desir miei,
ad altri no, ma a me sola vorrei,
ed iscolpirmi il tuo celeste velo,
qual fu quando dal Cielo
scendesti ad abitar la bassa terra
ed a tor l'uom di guerra.
Questa grazia, Signor, mi sia concessa
ch'io mostri col mio stil te a me stessa.

II

Lord, all merciful, who has until now
made me despise all mortal beauty
with my frail, ephemeral sight,
make me inherit through grace such goodness
that with pure heart I will love only you,
forever, devotedly, despising all else before me,
and with such true affection that everyone
points me out as your faithful lover
in this imperfect world
which is nothing without your heavenly love
but a tempestuous sea wracked with storms.

Lord, who was fashioned by your own hand,
when every mind strives in vain
to catch your lovely human face in verse,
I write now only to express my desires,
only for myself, for no-one else,
to sculpt your heavenly body
as it was when you came down
from heaven to live on this base earth
and turn men away from war.
Grace me with that skill, Lord,
so I may reveal you to myself.

Signor, nel piano spazio di tua fronte
la bellezza del Ciel tutta scolpita
si scorge, e con giustizia insieme unita
de l'alta tua pietade il vivo fonte,
e le pie voglie a perdonarci pronte.
Ombre dei lumi venerandi e sacri,
di Dio bei simulacri,
ciglia, del cor fenestre, onde si mostra
l'alma salute nostra:
occhi che date al sol la vera luce
che per voi soli a noi chiara riluce!

Signor, cogli occhi tuoi pien de salute
consoli i buoni e ammonisci i rei
a darsi in colpa di lor falli rei;
in lor s'impara che cosa è virtute,
O mia e tutte l'altre lingue mute,
perchè non dite ancor de' suoi capelli,
tanto del sol più belli
quanto è più bello e chiaro egli del sole?
O chiome uniche e sole,
che, vibrando dal capo insino al collo,
di nuova luce se ne adorna Apollo!

Signor, da questa tua divina bocca
di perle e di rubini, escon di fore
dolci parole ch'ogni afflitto core
sgombran di duolo e sol piacer vi fiocca
e di letizia eterna ogni un trabocca.
Guancie di fior celesti adorne, e piane
a le speranze umane;
corpo in cui si rinchiuse il Cielo e Dio,
a te consacro il mio:
la mente mia qual ful la tua statura
con gli occhi interni già scorge e misura.

Lord, heaven's beauty can be seen
carved on your forehead's broad plain,
where the vital fount of justice
unites with great mercy
and your pious wish to grant us swift pardon.
Shadows lie over your noble, sacred lights,
beautiful images of God,
heart's windows
revealing our soul's salvation;
eyes that give the sun its true light,
that through you shines clearly only on us!

Lord, with your eyes full of salvation
console the good and admonish the guilty
so they admit the guilt of their sins ;
through them we learn virtue's meaning.
O my tongue, and all others mute like mine,
why not say more about his hair
more lovely than the sun
just as he is more lovely, more brilliant, than the sun?
O incomparable hair and sun
rippling down from head to neck
so that Apollo is adorned with new light!

Lord, from this, your divine mouth
of pearls and rubies, sweet words pour out
to heal the pain of every damaged heart,
and only pleasure showers down,
flooding everyone with eternal delight.
Cheeks adorned with heavenly flowers
invite human hope;
body containing Heaven and God,
to you I consecrate my own:
my mind saw what was your stature,
my inner eye now takes its measure.

Signor, le mani tue non dirò belle
per non scemar col nome lor beltade;
mani, che molto innanzi ad ogni etade
ci fabricar la luna, il sol, le stelle:
se queste chiare son, quai sarann elle?
Felice terra, in cui le sacre piante
stampar tant'orme sante!
a la vaghezza del tuo bianco piede
il Ciel s'inchina e cede.
Felice lei, che con l'aurate chiome
le cinse e si scarcò de l'aspre some!

Canzon, quanto sei folle,
poi che nel mar de la beltà di Dio
con sì caldo desio
credesti entrare! or c'hai 'l cammin smarrito
réstati fuor, chè non ne vedi 'l lito.

Lord, I will not call your hands beautiful
so as not to diminish their beauty by naming them;
long before time began
they built for us the sun and stars and moon:
if those are bright, how much more are your hands?
Happy land, where sacred steps
place so many holy footprints!
Heaven kneels and yields
before the delicacy of your pale foot.
Happy the one who with her golden hair
embraced those feet and was relieved of her heavy load!

Canzone, how crazy you are,
to think that you could enter the sea
of God's beauty with such burning desire!
Now that you have lost your way,
stay out of it, for you cannot see the shore.

III

Quel che gli giorni a dietro
noiava questa mia gravosa salma,
di star tra queste selve erme ed oscure
or sol diletta l'alma;
chè da Dio, sua mercè, tal grazia impetro,
che scorger ben mi fa le vie secure
di gire a lui furo de le inique cure.
Or, rivolta la mente a la Reina
del Ciel, con vera altissima umiltade,
per le solinghe strade
senza intrico mortal l'alma camina
già verso il suo riposo,
che ad altra parte il pensier non inchina
fuggendo il tristo secol sì noioso,
lieta e contenta in questo bosco ombroso.

Quando da l'oriente
spunta l'Aurora dol vermiglio raggio
e ne s'annuncia da le squille il giorno,
allora al gran messaggio
de la nostra salute alzo la mente
e lo contemplo d'alte glorie adorno
nel basso tetto, dove fea soggiorno
la gran Madre di Dio ch'or regna in Cielo.
Così, godendo nel mio petto umile,
a lei drizzo il mio stile,
e 'l fral mio vel di roze veste velo,
e sol di servir lei,
non d'altra cura, al cor mi giunge zelo,
seguendo la vestigia di colei
che dal deserto accolta fu tra i Dei.

III

    To be in these dark
and lonely woods in days gone by
used to burden my heavy body
but now only delights my soul;
for from merciful God I implore such grace
that he makes me see the right road clearly,
one that travels towards him, away from wickedness.
Now, with my mind turned
to the Queen of Heaven in devout humility,
my soul walks along solitary roads
far from human intrigue
already towards its rest.
My thoughts incline no other way;
they flee these sad and troubled times
in this shady wood, happy and at peace.

   When in the east
dawn breaks with scarlet rays
and heralds the day with bells,
then I raise my thoughts
to the messenger of our salvation
and I contemplate him adorned with high glories
under the modest roof that sheltered God's great Mother
who now reigns in heaven.
So, with joy in my humble breast,
I offer her my skill,
dressing my frail body in rough clothes,
my heart inspiring me only to serve her
I care for nothing more
but follow the example of one who
from out of the desert was received among the Gods.

Quando da poi furo sorge
Febo, che fa nel mar la strada d'oro,
tutta m'interna e l'allegrezza immensa
ch'ebbe del suo tesoro
quella che tanta grazia or a me porge;
ch'io la riveggio con la mente intensa
mirare il figlio in caritate accensa,
nato fra gli animai, con pio sembiante;
e del sangue che manda al petto il core
nodrire il suo Signore;
e scerno il duce de l'eterno amante
sotto povere veste
spregiar le pompe del vulgo arrogant,
colui che sol pregiò l'aspre foreste
e fu fatto da Dio tromba celeste.

Poi che 'l suo chiaro volto
alzando, da le valli scaccia l'ombra
il biondo Apollo col suo altero squardo,
un bel pensier m'ingombra;
parmi veder Giesù nel tempio, involto
fra Saggi, disputar con parlar tardo,
e lei, per ch'io d'amor m'infiammo ed ardo,
versar dagli occhi, per letizia, pianto.
Questi conforti contra i duri oltraggi
m'apportan questi faggi,
lungi schivando di sirene il canto;
chè per solinghe vie
il bel gioven, a Dio diletto tanto,
con le sue caste voglie e sante e pie
vide il sentier de l'alte ierarchie.

And when Phoebus rises up,
turning the sea into a street of gold,
I am infused with an immense joy
that arises from her treasure,
she who now grants me so much grace;
that through intense concentration I see her again,
with glowing devotion watching her son
who was born with holy aspect among the living
and from her blood that streamed from heart to breast
to nourish her Lord:
and I see the forerunner of the eternal lover,
dressed in rags, scorning the pomp
of the arrogant masses,
the one whom God made the heavenly trumpet
finding truth only in wild forests.

When the blond Apollo raises
his bright face and with his proud look
chases shadow from the valleys,
a brilliant thought overwhelms me.
I seem to see Jesus in the temple, surrounded
by wise men, debating in a calm voice,
and she, for whom I burn with passion,
sheds tears of joy.
These beech trees bring me comfort
rather than unbearable suffering
and I shun the distant sirens' song:
for on solitary roads
the lovely youth, so beloved by God,
with his holy, pious and chaste desires,
saw the path of the angelic choirs.

Alzato a mezzo il polo
il gran pianeta co' bollenti rai,
ch'uccide i fiori in grembo a primavera,
s'alcuno vide mai
crucciato il padre contra il rio figliuolo,
così contemplo Cristo, in voce altera
predicando, ammonir la plebe fera
e col cenno, del qual l'Inferno pave,
romper le porte d'ogni duro core,
cacciando il vizio fore.
Quanto ti fu a vedere, o Dea, soave
gli errori conversi in cenere
del caro figlio in abito sì grave?
Quanto beata fu chi le sue tenere
membra a Dio consacrò, sacrate a Venere?

E se l'eterno Foco
giunge tant'alto ch'al calar rimira
ti scorgo, o Signor mio, fra i tuoi fratelli
senza minaccie od ira
del tuo amore infiammargli a poco a poco,
e co' leggiardri detti e gravi e belli
render beati e pien di grazia quelli,
lor rammentando pur la santa pace.
La gioia del mio cor, ch'amo ed adoro,
contemplo fra coloro
che i santi esempi tuori raccoglie e tace.
O via dolce e spedita,
trovata già nel vil secol fallace;
e chi'l primiero fu, dal Ciel m'addita
sol de l'erèmo la tranquilla vita!

The great planet that with its scorching rays
slaughters flowers in the lap of spring
has risen to half-pole;
if anyone has ever seen
a father angered by his wicked son,
that is how I contemplate Christ when in a proud voice
he preaches, admonishing the hostile crowd
and, with a gesture at which hell trembles,
breaks open the door of every hard heart,
chasing vice out.
O Goddess, how sweet was it
to see errors converted to ashes
so gravely by your dear son?
How blessed was she who consecrated
her tender limbs, once dedicated to Venus, to God?

And when the eternal Fire
rises so high it looks towards its setting,
I watch you, O my Lord, among your brothers
without threats or anger
inflame them little by little with your love,
and with elegant, grave, beautiful sayings
render them blessed and full of grace,
reminding them too of holy peace.
Among them I contemplate
my heart's joy, whom I love and adore,
gathering holy examples, then falling silent.
O sweet gift of a trail found at last
in these vile, wicked times, when from heaven
he who went first shows me the tranquil life
is only that of the hermitage.

Per voi, grotta felice,
boschi intricati e rovinati sassi,
Sinno veloce, chiare fonti e rivi,
erbe che d'altrui passi
segnate a me vedere unqua non lice,
compagna son di quelli spirti divi,
c'or là su stanno in sempiterno vivi,
e nel solare e glorioso lembo
de la madre, del padre e del suo Dio
spero vedermi anch'io
sgombrata tutta dal terrestre nembo,
e fra l'alme beate
ogni mio bel pensier riporle in grembo.
O mie rimote e fortunate strate,
donde adopra il Signor la sua pietate!

Quanto disovre e scalda il chiaro sole,
canzon, è nulla ad un guardo di lei,
ch'è Reina del Ciel, Dea degli dei.

Because of you, happy cave,
tangled woods and shattered rocks,
swift-moving Sinni, clear springs and streams,
grasses trodden by the footprints of others
I am never permitted to see,
I walk beside those divine spirits,
now high above in eternal life
and in the sun-drenched glorious seat
of the mother, father and her God,
I hope to see myself as well,
entirely released from earth's dark cloud
and among the souls of the blessed
pouring into her lap all my purest thoughts.
O my remote paths, blessed with fortune,
where the Lord dispenses his mercy!

However much the bright sun reveals and warms,
canzone, it is nothing compared to one look from her,
Queen of Heaven, Goddess of the gods.

South

A white arrow flies south along a coastline
of beach, umbrellas scattered and sea all a-glitter;
the land broadens out, flattens, changes filter
to yellow earth, burnt crops, pumpkins pitched
awkwardly in harvested fields. The soft wingtips
of windfarms (here they call them Aeolian fields)
quiver in the breeze. Grapevines clutch fingers
side by side on the flat, instead of grappling
on hills; white egrets crowd on a branch
arced over a river inlet. Mist becomes sun.

The train's twenty-five minutes late.
At Foggia travellers alight. The ticket collector,
hat askew, steps out, smokes a cigarette.
A horn announces departure. The arrow flies on
past ruined houses in unploughed fields, fallen
roofs on oblong brick *masserie,* past concrete bridges,
warehouses, apartment blocks, polytunnels and
African men, women in long skirts and headwraps,
bent double to pick tomatoes with trailing stems
for our *pastes* and *purées,* our *passatas,* our *pomo d'oro.*

CM

Tricarico

Rocco Scotellaro. In old photographs
he's by the side of the peasants
occupying the land, a 'poet of the people'

who travelled north for work but still
yearned for his homeland and whose poems
tolled the lives of the stricken south.

In Rabata, Giuseppe sits on his front step,
pulls the photo he still carries everywhere
out of his wallet, wipes away tears

remembering the injustices done
to Rocco, his friend, and his early death.
His wife behind him on a wooden chair

tells how the poet loved to dance
at her sister's parties and how he played
the game of *morra* into the night.

I've spread out the map of Lucania
on my kitchen table, each place-name
brings me one of his poems: the Bruna's

cavalcade and peasant saints of Matera;
a Potenza evening; Gravina gorge; the road to
Montescaglioso where Novello fell at dawn;

the twin lakes of Monticchio: two eyes
reflecting the sky, and in the distance
the volcanic crater of the Vulture.

CM

Some things remain the same

Change and change again. Romans, Saracens,
Albanians, Normans, each conquered in their turn.
Franciscans and Benedictines kneeled on the floor tiles
of Greek Orthodox monasteries; Christian mystics
and troubadours trod paths led by Sufis; the cult
of the Virgin Mary echoed that of Nizami's Layla
who was born in a tale from ancient Persia.

An hour's walk from Favale pilgrims crossed
the valley to the spot where a deer stood unharmed
by a hunter's arrow and an abbey was founded.
Occult signs marked castle walls. In every forest
and cave were sanctuaries, miraculous springs,
appearances, reliquaries. Devotion in exchange
for divine intervention. Crusades set off

to conquer Jerusalem; Spaniard fought French
for the Kingdom of Naples. Baronial families
expanded their territories (the San Severino clan
owned lands from Favale to Tricarico);
fields and serfs were bought and sold.
From Isabella to Rocco, four hundred years:
only the peasants' misery remained unchanged.

CM

From Tricarico to Favale

Westward now! Across the land from Adriatic to Ionian sea,
from Tricarico via Grassano, south of Matera towards Pisticci,
the town stretched like a white leopard across the hills, into
the *calanchi,* lunar landscape: pale striations, furrows deepening;

ridges scribbled with sage, myrtle and juniper, scaley skin tufted
with scrub; down snaking valleys through yellow clay mounds
sculpted by dry summers and torrential rains: deforestation, erosion.

I'm searching for Isabella. Everywhere I have found Rocco:
in his friends' memories, in Levi's painted tryptich in Matera,
in a statue in Tricarico's piazza, in photos on family walls

but Isabella is faceless. There exists no painting, no sketch.
Her burial place was not marked, so I search for her features
in the landscape she made hers. Every place has a story to tell.
In Favale Isabella hurled her poems from her castle on the hill.

CM

Scirocco

Who will ever hear me?
Only the African wind

drying up riverbeds
and killing seeds in the soil.

How it pounds the heat
against our stone walls!

Who will hear me?
Only wind from the south

filtering desert sand
between slats of shutters,

layering dust on our chairs,
skimming over flagstones.

Who will hear me?
Only Scirocco,

snatching verses
out of my hands

spinning them until they fall.
Who will ever hear me?

CM

'You say I'm not like others'

Yet surely, am I not like the peasant
who coaxes the smallest shoot from the earth?
He sets out at dawn, toils under the sun
and must return the next day and the next

to coax the smallest shoot from the earth
living in hope that rain will come
and still must return the next day and the next.
Brothers – we live in a hard land,

living in hope that rain will come,
far from the culture of the court of Naples.
Brothers –we live in a hard land,
so far from our father living in France,

so far from the culture of the court of Naples.
Where's the harm when I climb Monte Coppolo
(so very far from our father living in France)
and look down from the mountains across the ocean?

Where's the harm when I climb Monte Coppolo
and pour into my poems all my desires,
look down from the mountains across the ocean
with all I have felt and seen? Who else feels the pain

when I pour into my poems all my desires
after I've hurled my hopes from cliff-tops
with all I have felt and seen? Who else feels the pain
when even my poems abandon me

and I hurl my hopes from cliff-tops,
my voice hides away in caves with the owls
and even my poems abandon me,
and I could swear they will never return?

My voice hides away in caves with the owls,
while he sets out at dawn to toil under the sun,
and I could swear it will never return.
Surely, am I not like the peasant?

CM

A branch in the River Sinni

Trapped in lichen-
covered rocks
half-forked in the air

then relinquished
to bob beside a dead pike
over pearled pebbles

twined in weed
somersaulted
through torrents

the bark torn
stripped of leaves
bold wood cracked

the branch sways
dismembered
pushed onwards

streaked with
spume and grime
the stuff of waste.

She catches her breath,
over such waters
how can her voice be heard?

CM

Other days

I watch you lift your skirts,
climb up through forest paths,

pick your way over rocks at dawn
towards the peak of Monte Coppolo

before the heat descends,
and take your place on the hollowed stone

with only beetles and lizards for company,
from where you can see water

gleaming through the hills
but no sign of your father's ship.

There, viewing the abandoned land,
you're aware of your solitude.

But are there not days when you return,
your arms full of broom,

mind bursting with poems,
heart light as the new sky?

CM

Outside the wall

Iron bars on your window. You can just see
the courtyard below, terracotta pots

with geraniums and basil, cactus plants
against the brick, a strip of sunlight

across the cobbles and the tabby kitten
sprawled on warm stone.

There's a clatter of pans and dishes
from the kitchen, your mother is shouting

at the servants; a tap at the door
and Delfina brings your freshly laundered

petticoats and a word before she leaves.
Outside the wall at sunrise

you watched a line of men with their hoes
and shovels set off for the fields.

In the evening they'll return silent,
heads bowed, their steps slower.

You return to your desk and take up your pen.
The nib scratches the page and the plume

lifts in the draft from your window
carrying you to the French court,

to your brother, Scipione, and father,
to a place of *pavane* and *volta*.

CM

Fava

Tear open the downy pod when
the *fava* bean tastes of spring

– creamy green, fresh-born,
a breath of early morning air –

bed its coolness on your tongue
before the first bite and even if

it's old and wrinkled toss it in a pot
to tumble with onion and carrot,

garlic and celery and a *passata*
of last summer's ripe tomatoes

for sustenance throughout winter.
Try to forget what the ancients

warned you, that *fava* beans
contain the souls of the dead.

CM

Lemons

He brought your mother lemons from Amalfi,
called them Fruits of Paradise but warned her

the seed wouldn't grow on such stony ground.
She planted the pips and watered them daily

even after he'd gone and the lemon tree grew tall
under your window. At night the blossom's scent

would permeate your pillow and you'd remember
how the fruit held the colour of the new sun

while its skin stayed cool against your cheek in
summer heat. She blended the juice with honey,

serving each of you the sweet liquid in painted
terracotta bowls, its bitter taste disguised.

CM

The scattering

The guinea fowl's flown over
the fence down to a copse below.

While the farmer stomps the track
with his dog to flush her out

his wife remains, squeezing tight
under her arm another fowl,

his plump body pearled with muted
stars, to call the female back.

I'm told these birds mate for life.
With such despair he screeches!

– and the rest of the flock now
joins in with squawking crescendo.

Dusk closes the search;
the wood below turns quiet.

By morning, near the fence,
a flutter of feathers, scattering.

CM

'On my brothers' return from the hunt'

Shotguns on their shoulders,
they stumbled through the gate.
They'd left at midnight, were back
at sunrise, all of us out in the forecourt
to greet them. A horn sounded

and servants brought wine. First
came Decio and Fabio, then Marcantonio
with Cesare, a boy still, this his first hunt,
and the hounds bounded alongside,
blood fresh in their nostrils,

the youngest, Lupo, in the lead
weaving between the horses.
The night, they said, was black as sin
but both the dog and Cesare
had proved their mettle

and I thought – seeing my brother
stand there like a man, curls
damp around his face –
that he'd live up to his noble name.
Marcantonio held one end

of the shaft, Fabio the other.
The corpse hung from its feet,
snout and tusks to the ground,
leaving its stain on the stones behind.
'See the size of its *coglioni*',

Decio shouted and slapped the boy's head,
'Show us your trophy – *forza*, Cesare'.
When they killed a sow in error
my brothers would often bring me
one of her litter as a playmate

and the boar piglet, pale stripes
on its coat, would skip behind me
like a lapdog until, before it grew too big,
at my request they'd set it free.
This time, though, it was a male they'd shot.

Then Cesare threw down his sack,
tipped the thing out, head detached
from body, neck slashed
and, raucous with wine,
they each recounted the chase,

how nearly the striped youngster
had escaped, Cesare's headlong fall
to block its run, how he hacked
five times at its neck with his knife,
and its final scream.

CM

For honour's sake

Who was complicit
in Isabella's murder
and that of Don Diego,
her supposed lover?
Which brother,
Decio or Fabio, Marcantonio,
Cesare or Camillo?
It won't have been
Porzia her little sister
nor the older brother
Scipione (in France
with her father),
not the curate, her teacher
(they killed him too)
but it was the uncles,
Baldassino
and Cornelio,
not her mother
Luisa, powerless
to stop them.
And her dear beloved
father, Giovan Michele,
while writing his poetry
in the French king's court,
per conservationem honorem
did he approve
the murders
by Cesare, Decio, Fabio,
Cornelio, Baldassino?

CM

After Isabella's death, her mother curses

When they spoke to me of Honour
I cursed them and they called me mad.

The moon tonight is low and red.
Down in the piazza, sounds from *lira*

and *zampogna* tear the air like teeth.
I am poisoned by the spider

and will dance the tarantella,
I'll don a mask, join the gypsies

and despite my ancient bones I'll dance.
Faster than their drums, I'll dance.

CM

Notes

Sonnet V
Luigi refers to Luigi Alamanni, a famous poet who was with Isabella's father at the French court. Isabella hoped that Francis, King of France (1494–1547) would help her join her father.

Sonnet VI
King Francis 1 was defeated at the battle of Crépy (1544).

Canzone I
Caesar refers to Charles V, Spanish Emperor of the Kingdom of the Two Sicilies.

Fava
It is said that the village Favale was named after the *fava* beans growing in the surrounding fields.

Acknowledgements

For my translations I have relied mainly on Adele Cambria's *Isabella, la triste storia di Isabella Morra. Le Rime della poetessa di Valsinni* with very helpful notes and commentary by Giovanni Caserta. Edizioni Osanna Venosa (2003) and for background information, Giovanni Caserta's *Isabella Morra e la società meridionale del 500*, Edizioni Meta, Matera, 1976.

I am grateful to Vito Sacco for his kind hospitality in Tricarico and for driving me to Valsinni; to Vincenzo Rinaldi, the current owner of the castle where Isabella once lived, for showing me round the castle, now his home, and for providing enlightening information about her life and times; and to Cllr. GiuseppeTruncellito (*Assessore alla cultura*) and Carmen Chierico, from the *Pro Loco* (Visitors' Centre) of Valsinni, for advice, guidance and literature.

Thanks also to the *Centro delle Traduzioni, Biblioteca di Roma* whose facilities I was able to use when working on my initial drafts of the translations.

Isabella's Sonnet VII in English and ten of my own poems from this collection have appeared in *Long Poem Magazine*.

Many poet friends have offered me advice and encouragement on this collection which I have always appreciated. In particular, I would like to thank Mimi Khalvati, Ruth Valentine, Mandy Pannett, Olivia McCannon and Owen Gallagher.